X GAMES

BMX Park

by Connie Colwell Miller

Reading Consultant:
Barbara J. Fox
Reading Specialist
North Carolina State University

Content Consultant:
Keith Mulligan, Editor
Transworld Ride BMX magazine
Tustin, California

Capstone
press
Mankato, Minnesota

Blazers is published by Capstone Press,
151 Good Counsel Drive, P.O. Box 669, Mankato, Minnesota 56002.
www.capstonepress.com

Library of Congress Cataloging-in-Publication Data
Miller, Connie Colwell, 1976–
    BMX Park / by Connie Colwell Miller.
    p. cm.—(Blazers. X games.)
    Includes bibliographical references and index.
    ISBN-13: 978-1-4296-0105-4 (hardcover)
    ISBN-10: 1-4296-0105-1 (hardcover)
    1. Bicycle motocross—Juvenile literature. 2. ESPN X-Games—Juvenile
literature. I. Title. II. Series.
GV1049.3.M55 2008
796.6'2—dc22   2007001739

Summary: Describes the sport of BMX Park, focusing on the X Games,
including star athletes.

Essential content terms are bold and are defined at the bottom of the page where they first appear.

Editorial Credits
Mandy R. Robbins, editor; Bobbi J. Wyss, designer; Jo Miller, photo researcher

Photo Credits
AP/Wide World Photos/Branimir Kvartuc, 6, 7, 8; Ed Reinke, 27;
    Mark J. Terrill, cover, 18, 26; Paul Sakuma, 24–25
Corbis/Bo Bridges, 21; NewSport/Steve Boyle, 10–11, 16–17, 28–29
Getty Images Inc./Jeff Gross, 22–23; Lisa Blumenfeld, 4–5
ZUMA Press/Vaughn Youtz, 12, 13, 14, 15

1 2 3 4 5 6 12 11 10 09 08 07

Table Of Contents

Busting BMX Tricks

In August 2006, fans swarmed the X Games bicycle motocross (BMX) **course** in Los Angeles. Scotty Cranmer was just beginning his run.

course (KORSS)—a set path that athletes compete on

Cranmer worked the **obstacles**.
He launched into a 360 double-tailwhip.
Then he flipped completely over, turning
his bike around at the same time.

obstacle (OB-stuh-kuhl)—an object such as a
ramp or box jump that BMX riders do tricks on

When Cranmer landed, the fans went wild. The awesome tricks he busted earned him the gold medal in BMX park.

BLAZER FACT

When BMX bikers get hurt, they call their scabs "bacon."

BMX Park Basics

BMX park riders compete at skateparks. They use rails, ramps, and other obstacles to do tricks on their bikes.

Morgan Wade

Colin MacKay

BMX park riders grind rails and do **stalls**. These tricks use the pegs that stick out from the wheels of their bikes.

stall (STAHL)—to pause on one wheel of a bike and balance for a length of time

Ryan Nyquist

pegs

Colin MacKay

Park riders don't just do tricks on the ground. They use ramps and pipes to perform **aerials**. They let go of parts of their bikes while flying through the air.

aerial (AIR-ee-uhl)—a trick done while soaring through the air

Competing in Park

Park competitions have two rounds. In the first round, each rider takes two runs. Judges give each rider a score from 70 to 100.

Ryan Nyquist

Steve McCann

BMX Park judges rate competitors on style and originality. The 10 best riders move on to the final round. These riders take another two runs. In the final round, the top rider wins.

BLAZER FACT

Riders have 60 to 90 seconds to show their moves.

Winners earn cash prizes called purses. BMX purses are often thousands of dollars. But to BMX riders, the pride in winning is worth more than money.

Dave Mirra

BMX Park Diagram

quarter pipe

ramp

quarter pipe

wedge

maxell

23

BMX Records

Dave Mirra holds an impressive 14 gold medals in the X Games. Four of these medals are in BMX park.

BLAZER FACT

In 1995, Dave Mirra tore his spleen in half while throwing a trick.

Ryan Nyquist trails Mirra with 12 X Games gold medals. Nyquist has been competing in BMX since 1996. He wows fans with big tricks like his no-footed can-can barspin.

Ryan Nyquist

Dave Mirra

Riders like Mirra and Nyquist helped create the tricks that today's riders bust. Young riders continue to practice their sport. Fans count on them to keep BMX park exciting year after year.

Rockin' a tailwhip!

Glossary

aerial (AIR-ee-uhl)—a trick that is done in the air

course (KORSS)—a set path; BMX riders compete on courses with obstacles, jumps, and turns.

motocross (MOH-toh-kross)—a sport in which people race motorcycles on dirt tracks

obstacle (OB-stuh-kuhl)—an object that BMX riders do tricks on

originality (uh-ri-juh-NAH-luh-tee)—being new and unusual

stall (STAHL)—when a rider pauses briefly, balancing on an obstacle

Read More

Dick, Scott. *BMX*. Radical Sports. Chicago: Heinemann, 2003.

Fiske, Brian D. *BMX Events*. BMX Extreme. Mankato, Minn.: Capstone Press, 2004.

Mugford, Simon. *Essential BMX*. Twenty4Sevens. New York: Tangerine Press, 2004.

Internet Sites

FactHound offers a safe, fun way to find Internet sites related to this book. All of the sites on FactHound have been researched by our staff.

Here's how:
1. Visit *www.facthound.com*
2. Choose your grade level.
3. Type in this special code **1429601051** for age-appropriate sites. You may also browse subjects by clicking on letters, or by clicking on pictures or words.
4. Click on the **Fetch It** button.

FactHound will fetch the best sites for you!

Index